Tourist or Pilgrim?

Also by Margaret Clark and published by Ginninderra Press
Frayed Edges

Margaret Clark

Tourist or Pilgrim?

Acknowledgements

My thanks go to my writing companions, my friends, my church family and my biological family. Thanks, too, to many strangers around the world who turned out to be friends I just hadn't met before. All are a source of inspiration for my poetry and love in my life.

Much gratitude to Stephen and Brenda at Ginninderra Press, who have given me the opportunity to fulfil a long-held dream of sharing my words with a broader audience.

Special thanks to my husband, my ever patient husband, who puts up with being read to and written about with great composure and is also a wonderfully honest critic and proofreader.

Love to you all.

Some poems in this collection have been previously published in the following anthologies and magazines:
'Passion of the Trinity', *No Strings Attached*,
Eremos Poetry Anthology, 1999;
'Apples and Snakes' and 'The Modem and I', *Worlds in Words*,
Friendly Street Poets Anthology 41, 2017;
'The Light of Reason', *The Guardian Magazine*,
Anglican Diocese of Adelaide, Easter 2018;
'Why is it Father?', *It's Still All Write*, JYC Anthology 3, 2018;
'Oxford', 'Tourist or Pilgrim?' and 'A Cold Day in Summer',
Dream-Water Fragment, Friendly Street Poets Anthology 42, 2018.

Tourist or Pilgrim?
ISBN 978 1 76041 633 1
Copyright © text Margaret Clark 2018
Cover image and artwork by Margaret Clark
Photograph of the dancers, page 38, by Alyssum Jade Photography
All other internal images by Margaret and Nigel Clark

First published 2018 by
GINNINDERRA PRESS
PO Box 3461 Port Adelaide 5015
www.ginninderrapress.com.au

Contents

A World of Wonder	9
Praise be the Sky	11
Aristotle's Elements	12
Summer Days in Winter	14
Seasons of Life	15
Freedom in Three Dimensions	16
A Cold Day in Summer	18
Close to Home	19
Family	21
Why is it, Father?	22
The Cobweb Inspector	24
Farewell	26
Son	27
Daughter	28
Second child	29
Not a love poem	30
Husbands and Wives	32
Middle Child	34
How I Miss You	36
For a Lifetime	38
Going Home	40
Miss Alice	42
I Couldn't do it Without You	44
Honey	46
Musings	47
Dancing stars	49
Preparing to Write	50
The Tiny Poem	52
The Sonnet	53

Old Furniture	54
Writer's Block	56
Healing	59
Nocturne	60
Being a Poet	62

Tourist or Pilgrim? — 63

Travelling Light	65
Gone to See Ships	66
The Hand of a Mayan Child	69
So Hard to Stop	72
For Love and Other Cruises	74
Lindisfarne	75
Tourist or pilgrim?	76
Oxford	78
The Artisans	80

Questions of the Soul — 83

Tapestry	85
This Light of Reason	86
The Depth of Unknowing	88
To Grasp the Infinite	89
The Passion of the Trinity	90
The Precious Gem	92
Apples and Snakes	93

Insecurities and Doubts — 95

Blemishes	97
No Pictures Please	98
Always the Bridesmaid	99
Self e-steam	100
Hollow	101
Islands of Humanity	102
Insecurities	103

Resignation	104
When you are away	105
Each day is a gift	106
Living in the Shade	107
On the Lighter Side	**109**
Buying Local	111
The Modem and I	112
Oh, I Wish I Hadn't Eaten That	114
Exotics	115
On the Soapbox	117
The Den	119
Carbon Footprint	120
Best We Forget	121
You Are Homeless	122
Questions of the Night	124
Upon the Merest Hint	126
Semaphore, the End of the Line	127

A World of Wonder

Praise be the sky of night
a dome of indigo
that wraps the world
in wonder

Praise be the Sky

Praise be the sky of night,
a dome of indigo
that wraps the world
in wonder,

lit by lanterns
from the heavens.

Praise be the moon
that guides the tides
and breathes life into being.

Praise be the stars
that guide the sailors
over oceans,
and wise men to their destiny,

As the world turns,
the dome fades pale
to softest pinks and blues.

Praise be our glorious sun
the source of light
and life.

Aristotle's Elements

We live with the elements,
nourished by their gifts.
Rest by the hearth on a winter's night.
Sail by the currents and the winds.
Slake our thirst with life-giving water.

Fire, wind and water;
we capture them with our solar panels,
turbines and dams.

We think we have won,
harnessed them
for our own means.

Shallow victory indeed.

They turn capricious.
Savage with bush fire and volcano.
Grow in anger to a hurricane,
or leave the sailor becalmed at sea.
Inundate with flood or withdraw with drought.

Such elemental beasts cannot be tamed.

Meanwhile, the translucent ether,
more subtle than light, holds us safe,
ever bound within the dark matter,
the crystalline sphere of orbit
round the sun.

But what of the earth, the stoic earth?
She does not cry when we walk upon her face
nor bleed when we scar and furrow to plant our grain.
She holds no protest as we dig deep
to steal her jewels and minerals.
Holds silent as we degrade her with our waste,
bury our dead, deep within her heart.
The earth, the stoic earth;
when will she turn, and say, 'No more'?

Summer Days in Winter

A brief reprieve from the cold
and grey of winter.
Gentle warmth and blue skies
kiss the morning air.

A gift to lift the spirits,
ease the aching joints
and cold bones
from winter's melancholia.

Let me escape the indoors,
feel the sun's rays
upon my skin,
see the contrast of light and shade.

Birds sing with joy
at this brief winter gift.
Bare branches
feel the sap rise.

And yet there is a sting
in this brief summer tale.
Clear skies of day
bring cold skies of night.

No cloud to quilt the heavens.

And morning frosts burn
the fresh green buds
teased out by warmth and light
of these false summer days.

Seasons of Life

Spring

> At birth a helpless creature, needing, crying.
> At two a wayward changeling, testing, trying.
> By five, a tiny glimpse of independence,
> uniforms, new shoes and school attendance.

Summer

> Adolescent angst to adulthood,
> getting jobs and buying food.
> Sharing flats and living rough.
> Houses, cars and other stuff.

Autumn

> Children grow, the mortgage shrinks.
> Blood pressure rises, passion sinks.
> Jobs, romances, bodies – all are tired,
> a life of busyness and things acquired.

Winter

> The waist grows thick, the hair grows thin.
> We think of things that might have been.
> We now have time to smell the flowers
> Relax the mind, and squander hours.
>
> Was it worth it all, this gathering of things?
> Then grandkids come, and lead us back to spring.

Freedom in Three Dimensions

I walk along the shoreline
enjoying the breeze and the sound of waves.

Just out from the shore,
a pod of dolphins inscribe graceful arches
slicing the air with their dorsal fins
and diving again to the watery deep.

A squadron of corellas, soar overhead
squawking and competing
as they fly.
Beautiful creatures, pale pink and white
against the blue winter sky,
the light shimmering
through the translucent edges
of their outstretched wings.

I envy these creatures,
their effortless movements.
What a joy to be able to fly or swim,
such freedom in three dimensions,
to wheel and dance
among the thermals and currents.

We humans, grounded,
have lost a dimension
granted to those who live
in water or air.

We have the brain power,
we have done the science,
devised the aerofoil theory of lift,
learnt to make machines
to lift us high or dive us deep.

It is not the same though
as the freedom
of God's creature's
who can move in air or water
with feather or fin.

A Cold Day in Summer

January 2013

There's something about days like this
that take the music out of summer.
The birds don't congregate around the bird bath.

The clouds are in monochrome.
No hint of gold or lilac.
The sun has hardly shown its face all day.

And when it does, the garden
is hardened in sharp shadows,
with no warmth in the bright light.

The wind sighs instead of sings.
Flowers have lost their colour,
insects, their sense of purpose.

It is all wrong, lifeless, lukewarm.
Give me summer heat or winter cold.
Let each season wear its own attire.

Close to Home

'At the touch of love
everyone becomes a poet'
– Plato

Family

family
a diaspora of diverse souls
spread across a continent, a world
so different in talent, tastes
and temperaments
yet bound
in twist of DNA
in turn of phrase
commonality of memory
and mannerism

family
who make a point
of gathering the clan
of coming together in kindness
to mark the milestones
and the rites of passage
so thank you all
for being you
for being us.

Why is it, Father?

On the 40th anniversary of your passing, September 2016

Why is it, Father,
that I have never before
written a poem for you?

It must be time
to put aside my notions
of your severity,
your frugality of affection,
your paucity of praise.

Find the real you.

I need to remember the man
who laboured with his children
over maths and physics,
corrected their grammar
and spelling.

You taught us never
to be content with
'I don't know.'

You took us on safari
through encyclopaedia,
atlas and dictionary,
in search of answers,
long before search engines
were invented

You were the enquiring mind,
the lover of books and knowledge,
the believer in education.

A father who pushed his girls
as hard as his boys.

You were quiet,
a little too serious, perhaps,
but my role model
for honesty, integrity
and hard work.

Thank you, Father
for teaching me
the love of learning.

The Cobweb Inspector

When she was in her prime
she ran the accounts department
of a huge dairy cooperative.

Always smart and on the go.
A fastidious housekeeper
a keen cook and gracious hostess.

She knitted for her large family,
cared for her ageing father.
Nothing was too much trouble.

She gave her daughters-in-law
a hard time.
They could never measure up
to her high standards.

She was dubbed
'the cobweb inspector',
a joke she was happy to share.

'When I get to heaven,'
she'd laugh,
'I'll change all the sheets
and tidy the cupboards.'

In her eighties now,
she sits alone, watching soapies
and eating TV dinners.
Seeks no company, besides her cat.

How I wish she had
the gregarious nature,
the feisty spirit,
of her younger days.

Too shaky to knit, she says,
too blind to read,
and the only cobwebs she sees
are in her mind.

Farewell

8 April 2014

I said my final farewell today
to someone I hardly knew,
the mother of an old school friend,
and yet I met her over fifty years ago.

Why do we wait till death
to celebrate a life?

To find that the housewife
and mother from Southend
joined the Wrens as a young girl,
flew with test pilots in the war.

Defended her home land
in word and deed.
Demonstrated against the hypocrisy
of the church.

Earned a degree in mathematics
when her children were grown.

How could I know,
when she let me play chopsticks
on her precious piano,
that she could play Chopin?

Why do we wait for a eulogy
to declare
there is no such thing
as an ordinary life?

Son

Nearly twenty-five,
pumps iron, runs marathons.
Good shoulders, great thighs.
My very own Iron Man.

He grins and strikes a pose.

I smile
remembering the boy of three
sternly tell his baby sister
'Girls don't need muscles.'

I laugh and shake my head
clear of the vision
and love him as I always will.

For under the slightly
chauvinist veneer
is a kind, gentle man
who respects women.

Reveres his lovely wife
and still loves his sister
and his mum and dad.

I thank God for him
just as he is.
I ask no more of this my son.

Daughter

I hold my daughter close,
not a child now, but a grown woman
inches taller than me
and a buxom wench to boot.

I hold her away, better to drink
with my senses
the straight blonde hair,
fair skin and grey-green eyes,
the figure of a woman in her bloom.

I can taste my pride in her
tinged with the sharp spice of regret
at my own passing years
and the time we spend apart.

Married now and thriving on it.
Overflowing with life and good humour.
Madly in love with her man
and filled with an exuberant passion for God.

I send a prayer of gratitude to Heaven
'My goodness, Lord,
you and I have done a wonderful job.'

Second child

The excitement
of the first born
worn, expended.

This birth was easy;
it's all been done before,
a little short of miracle
the second time around.

It will always be like this;
second walk and second words
fewer photographs
and pre-loved clothes.

The older sister;
she will always be there
blazing trails.
Comparison and compromise
to make you stumble.

Be yourself,
our dark-haired beauty,
for second-born
does not mean second-best.

Not a love poem

I was asleep when you turned in, turned on
the light, the tap. Flushed, washed, brushed,
and trampolined onto the bed.

I was almost asleep again
when your cold hands roamed into regions
of my topography which require a permit,
even for the regular visitor.

I was awake when you turned away, angry,
because I just wanted to sleep,
and only minutes later when your breathing
slowed and deepened.

I was awake when a rain squall came through
and painted white noise on the roof,
and when the moon came out from behind the clouds,
forcing its light, thin-sliced, through the blinds.

I was awake when you rolled on your back,
your profile backlit and your breathing heavy.

I was awake when the sky darkened again, the moon hidden
behind cloud, or travelling west. We are not close these days,
the moon and I, since I no longer pedal her lunar cycle.

I was awake when a cricket soloist outside the window
joined the tinnitus choir inside my head
and when you snored so loudly you half woke yourself
and turned on your side, silent, with just a gentle nudge from me.

I was awake when the sky paled, in another grey cliché
of early morning light.

I was asleep until you put your hand on my shoulder,
warm this time, and said you were sorry,
as though you had turned away only moments before.

And I'm sorry that I tossed and turned all night
while you slept.

I'm sorry too that you think it's okay to wake me.
Because it isn't, and the answer is still 'No.'

Husbands and Wives

'Wives submit to your husbands as is fitting in the Lord
Husbands, love your wives and do not be harsh with them.'
– Colossians 3:18–19, Ephesians 5:22

Admit it!
He's bigger, stronger, at least physically,
and history has given him the upper hand.

But who bears the children,
copes with dirty nappies and midnight feeds,
sleep deprivation and sick children?

But who's now liberated?

You mean to juggle the kids, the housework
and a job?

We both have strengths and weaknesses
but marriage is not a contest.

It's not about who picks up the socks
or picks up the tab,
who changes the bed
or changes the tyre.

It's about love, the Jesus kind,
open, honest and giving.

It's about spending a life
with your best friend.
Sharing the tough times
and the good.

Bending, so you won't break.

Where home is a safe haven,
a glimpse of heaven in a fallen world.

It's about being on the same team,
being each other's greatest fan,
cheering each other on.

And it's meant to be fun.

Marriage is God's idea
where two become one flesh,
where two together can achieve
so much more than two apart.

Marriage is God's idea
with only one rule:
love the other as you love yourself.
It is that simple and that hard.

Middle Child

I was born in the middle of the century,
in the middle of England, a middle child,
in Midhouse in the Hollow.
Just Mum and me,
no one else around, not even the midwife.

But no one starts life as a middle child.
There is, for a while,
that favoured position of youngest.

And for me there were four glorious years
playing on my frailties,
before my world was shattered
by a baby brother.

Soon after, I was packed
off to school, rejected and resentful.
And then another one, another boy arrived,
not even a little sister.

Where was Mum getting them from?

So now the symmetry was set in concrete.
Two above me, two below.
Two with grown-up privileges,
two with no apparent consequences.

And me, in the middle.
Old enough to do dishes.
Not old enough to play out late.
Big enough to know better.
Not big enough to do things by myself.

And still when I am with them
the feelings arise, the hierarchy exists,
but only in my mind, I think,
not theirs.

So now that four of us
have reached our seventh decade,
and one has slipped serenely into her eighth,
it may be time to admit
they're not to blame
for making me a middle child.

How I Miss You

1998 – for my first grandchild who lived too far away

How I miss you
little girl,
growing up
while I'm away.

I want to see you smile.
See the crawling
and the first
wobbly steps.

I want to be there
for a cuddle
when the teeth
are being mean.

I want to see
ice cream
and spinach
on your chin.

Hear the laughter
and the first words,
the cacophony of
saucepan lids
and wooden spoons
on the kitchen floor.

Share the stories at bedtime
as eyelids grow heavy:
watch your head
sink in a cloud
of happily ever after.

For a Lifetime

8 December 2017, my granddaughter's wedding day

It is time now for the 'happily ever after'

She is getting married that little girl.
A child no longer, a young woman
with so much beauty, love
and happiness in her eyes.

She faces her man and
they promise to love and cherish
with the understanding
there will be good times
and bad.

Promise to be quick to forgive
and ask for forgiveness.

In the dappled light of the forest,
and in the sight of God,
they share the bread and wine,
the body and blood of our Lord,
just the two of them.

They wash each other's feet
as a sign of service and honour
to one another

They have the blessing
and loving support
of friends, family
and the church.

As individual
strands of humanity
we can so easily break.

Twist us together
in a three-strand chord,
man, woman and God,
and there will be love
and strength enough
to last a lifetime.

Going Home

I travelled halfway round the world
to find my birthplace
a tiny row cottage
in a tiny village
where my mother alone,
brought me into the world.

Where the midwife
arrived too late
and believed I wouldn't make it.

Where the clergyman said
he must baptise me at once
so, if worst came to worst
I could be buried in hallowed ground.

But mother and I
were stronger than that
and she sent him packing
with his dodgy theology.

There would be no baptism.
Nor did she need
the shoe box she said
she would bury me in
if 'worst came to worst'.

And now I am back
at Midhouse in the Hollow
over sixty years later.
Some one else's home
someone else's story.

No one is home.
No one to talk to.
No door to knock on.

For the worst thing now is
that there are only two cottages.
The Midhouse has been swallowed
by the end cottage.

And where the front door was,
there is a brick infill,
the lintel still there to reveal its history.
So I stand before this brick barrier,
this masonry metaphor for life,
that says there is no turning back.

Miss Alice

My final grandchild, I think

You are a new life, Miss Alice,
and from the day
you came into the world
I could discern the features
of your sister, your father
and your great aunt.

In you is continuity;
a new bud, a new branch
on our gnarled old family tree.

And now at two, you bring
fresh discovery to old hearts,
make new again the joy of life.

Hours spent in happy play
with something
as simple
as a blue balloon.

'Boing,' you say, 'boing'
as we bounce it to the ceiling.

We share so much,
you and I, Miss Alice.
Books, pictures
shapes, colours.

We build together
our architectural masterpieces
in multicoloured Lego,
learning words along the way;
window, wall, roof, door.

We both love Thomas
(Dylan or the Tank Engine).
We both look to the moon
and think of Buzz
(Aldrin or Lightyear)
and dream of infinity and beyond.

Even poetry we share
as I push you
ever higher on the swing
and you cry out with glee,
'Up high!
Fly in the sky!'
and wave your little arms
like wings.

Yes, Miss Alice, you are a new life
sharing our stories and our DNA,
but your spirit is all your own,
brand-new and growing day by day
and blessing us all
who can but love you.

I Couldn't do it Without You

For my wonderful man, August 2012

I wonder what I would have done with my life
if you hadn't come along.

Would I ever have moved from the familiarity of home,
seen other parts of the country and the world?

Would I have been brave enough to change professions in my thirties
without your help and encouragement?

You believed in me
when I had trouble believing in myself.

We have brought two beautiful children into the world
and swell with pride at the people they have become.

Life these days may not be as adventurous
as in our crazy youth

but I still need you around.

I need you to cook when I don't feel like cooking
to stop me living on chocolate and chips.

I need you to bring me cups of tea in bed
to get me moving in the mornings.

I need you to push me out of my comfort zone
when I would retreat into my shell.

I need you to be my eyes and nerves,
to drive me where I am not brave enough to go.

I need you to mess things up a bit
when I make tidiness more important than creativity.

I need you to share our good memories,
and not allow us to get grumpy and old.

To look after me if I am sick
(I'll do the same for you).

It's a good life
and I couldn't do it without you.

Honey

You call me honey,
the product of a stinging insect.
Am I both sweet
and dangerous?

You call me honey.
Do I stick to you too hard?
Wipe my sticky fingers
on your heart, your life?

But honey is food
for a family of hundreds,
food that lasts for centuries.

It is the product
of a creature
that works in community,
will sacrifice its life
for the common good.

Seeks beauty and
creates sweetness
and by some grand design,
turns flower into fruit.

Cross-pollinating, fertilising,
keeping the world alive.

Yes, you can call me honey.

Musings

Dancing stars

'One must have chaos in oneself to be able to give birth to a dancing star.' – Friedrich Nietzsche

Dreams and visions
fly around the universe
like dancing stars
searching for a host.

And should you be so blessed,
in symbiotic bond,
the seeds shall grow
until they're ready to be born.

Nurture and hold fast
in happy chaos
lest they escape
to seek
a more light-hearted soul.

Preparing to Write

If I want to write,
first I must tidy my desk,
all the papers neatly stacked,
pens and pencils in a little jar
or lined up in a military row.

A cup of tea or coffee perhaps
before I begin.
Might as well do the dishes
while the kettle boils.

I get any phone calls
out of the way
and pay the bills.

It is hard to settle
if I haven't made the bed
and the carpets
may need to be vacuumed.

Time to write.
I can multitask by putting on some washing,
that can happen while the creative juices flow.
I'll take a break later to hang it out.

Lunchtime, we creative types
have to remember to eat
and I have to pick up a few things
at the shop.

I get started on dinner
before the family comes home
to invade my head space.

Perhaps tomorrow…

At least the desk is tidy,
as neat and orderly as all the sonnets
I have yet to write.

The Tiny Poem

Written with Samuel Taylor Coleridge's quill, 12 May 2015
Coleridge's Cottage, Nether Stowey, Somerset

Let there be time
to sharpen
the quill and mind
and yet to soften
the heart and soul
in the gentle light
of a summer afternoon.

The Sonnet

From Wikipedia: 'A Shakespearean, or English, sonnet consists of 14 lines, each line containing ten syllables and written in iambic pentameter in which a pattern of an unstressed syllable followed by a stressed syllable is repeated five times. The rhyme scheme in a Shakespearean sonnet is a-b-a-b, c-d-c-d, e-f-e-f, g-g; the last two lines are a rhyming couplet.'

First quatrain: An exposition of the main theme and main metaphor.
Second quatrain: Theme and metaphor extended or complicated; often, some imaginative example is given.
Third quatrain: Peripeteia (a twist or conflict), often introduced by a 'but' (very often leading off the ninth line).
Couplet: Summarises and leaves the reader with a new, concluding image.

I ought to write a sonnet, 'fore I die
to claim to be a poet tried and true.
It can't be all that hard, I can but try
five feet, iambic beat and rhyming too.

I need a theme, a puzzlement to brood,
of love or justice, all the finer things,
or to something quite etherial elude,
or flippant things like cabbages and kings.

So what is it I feel I have to prove?
It isn't quite so easy after all.
Will Shakespeare's sonnets seem to flow so smooth
I feel my pen's not answering the call.

My muse has gone and left me all at sea.
I might give up and have a cup of tea.

Old Furniture

Inspired by Thomas Hardy's poem of the same name

I don't know how it may be with others
when the glossy catalogues arrive
stuffed in the letter box
to tempt and dissatisfy.

It is the furniture ones that get me in,
new lounges and fancy corner units,
extension tables and matching chairs,
posh little hall stands for the style zealots.

Things that match, how fine would that be.
A collection with some sort of theme
instead, this hotchpotch of
other people's pre-loved things.

An oak dresser bought from friends
returning to the States;
turned legs, carved drawers and doors,
a mirror trimmed in iron lace.

My favourite piece of furniture,
a little damaged, more's the pity,
with a chunk out of one corner
a memento of our move to the city.

A coffee table, once an old school desk,
sanded, varnished and lovingly restored,
its drawers full of books, pencils and puzzles
to keep my younger visitors employed.

Bookcases that look like they fell
off the back of a truck, because they did,
but hold a whole world of treasures
in history, art and the written word.

A bureau from a little antique shop
in Alice Springs, run by a friend of a friend,
filled with things of no great monetary value,
but memories that wealth transcends.

A gate-leg table, our one and only heirloom,
four generations in the family's hands,
fallen from genteel grace of afternoon teas
to the indignity of a printer stand.

The cheap pine desk I sit at now,
filled with ancient clutter (the desk and me),
painted once white, mustard and later faux timber,
its history shows where arms have come to rest.

It has witnessed the homework assignments
and tears of children now grown.
Suffered the angst of the would-be artist
and seen the birth of many poems.

I don't know how it may be with others,
browsing the catalogues of all things new and trendy,
but mostly I am content with my eclectic memories,
and furniture that has a story.

Writer's Block

A writer's block moved in
and set up camp within my special place.
But how could I describe it at the time?
Words would not come.

It wasn't like a butcher's block,
solid and practical.
No fine timber, sanded and scrubbed.

Nor was it dark and frightening
with knife marks and blood stains.
It was far too ethereal for that
and gentle as Morpheus.

So much smaller than I imagined
at the start, too low to sit at,
too nebulous to rest a laptop,
or even a notebook and pen.

It was made of mist,
soft, grey and never quite in focus.
Now and again I glimpsed
a hint of colour in my peripheral vision,
but I turned and it was gone.

Was I shrinking or was it growing?
It transfigured into
something far more threatening.
An infestation, not just a visitor.

It invaded my head and stole my words.
Crisp ideas melted from my thoughts
and it licked them like ice cream.
It crunched on the
peanut brittle of confidence,
savoured the sherbet fizz of inspiration.

As it ate,
the mist became a smog.

Ever hungry it drifted to my books,
singled out Roget's *Thesaurus*,
caressing the pages with its tongue,
swallowing slowly,
synonym by synonym.

Unsated, it made for
the *Oxford English Dictionary*,
stopping only briefly between volumes.
Worked its way through P to Z
Then A to O
until the pages were blank.

And then an eerie stillness.
Was it over?

It showed no interest in the
remainder of my modest library.

Only loose words, free words
appeared to be its taste.
No interest in those already
strung together in pearls of wisdom
or threaded casually into cheerful bling.

So there was hope.

For I could take those words,
from others' works,
copy them one at a time,
rearrange them into something new.

But I found it wasn't so.

Some were stuck fast in little phrases
that belonged to others.
And those I could set free
I couldn't string together.

Not only had it stolen all my words,
it had eaten up the thread.

Healing

A sonnet

The day you went away I gathered all
the tiny shattered pieces of my heart,
wrapped lovingly within a silken shawl,
for surely it can't mend while we're apart.

And then I carefully folded all my dreams
beside my heart, within a velvet case
and hid them high, the only way it seems
to make the memories of you erase.

Time heals and curiosity revives.
I lift the lid, too nervous to exhale.
I find my heart is scarred, but still alive
and yet the dreams seem very small and pale.

I try them on, but they no longer suit.
So brand-new dreams, I hope, will soon bear fruit.

Nocturne

September 1995

There's a lump in the mattress and a crease in the sheet
and the pillow's too soft and too old
I roll over in bed and the blankets fall off
and my feet and my kidneys are cold.

The warm body beside me is peacefully sleeping
the sleep of an innocent boy,
still and content and evenly breathing
just loud enough to annoy.

I turn on my back but not for too long
till my neck and my tail bone are hurting.
I roll to the window, the street light's too bright.
Remind me to buy thicker curtains.

I peer over the body to look at the clock.
The eerie green light says it's two.
So I go to the toilet and get a quick drink
just for something to do.

I find a warm place to put my cold feet
and he turns and snuggles in near.
He kisses my cheek and says that he loves me
and proceeds to snore in my ear.

In my mind I write letters that'll never reach paper,
draw houses that no one will build
I try drifting on clouds, upward to heaven,
but earthbound, I'm adding up bills

I straighten the sheet and turn over the pillow
How good could the other side be?
The clock says it's four and that is a comfort.
It means I missed out on three.

Outside the wind builds and sounds like the surf.
Ah, imagine warm beaches, blue skies.
Relax and go with it.... Who am I kidding?
Well it feels like there's sand in my eyes.

The pillow is hard now, its worse than before
and the lump in the mattress has thickened.
The dogs in the street are having a bark-fest
and the cats are making more kittens.

Around five the sky greys and the roosters join in.
Ah, the cycle of day is eternal.
I sleep until nine and front late for work.
Perhaps I am really nocturnal

Being a Poet

Based on an excerpt from *The Afternoon of a Writer* by Peter Handke

There have been long droughts
of lethargy and laziness
when the words would not come.

The return is always slow and arduous,
each word on paper
appreciated, celebrated,
filling my lungs with life-giving air.

And the discipline of those few words
etched out each morning
keep away the melancholy and the demons,
make me invincible for yet another day.

Has the fear always been there
in writing, in life, in love?
A fear of commitment, of failure
of the long haul?

Writing had long been the dream,
but a little awkward to proclaim
when there is nothing to show for it.

So the drought had brought me resolution
of discipline and routine.
A thousand hours of words and perseverance
so I can say I am a poet.

Tourist or Pilgrim?

A change of scenery
or a change of heart?

Tourist or Pilgrim?

A change of scenery
or a change of heart?

Travelling Light

A terza rima

My suitcase once again reveals my lack
of any aptitude to travel light,
or make the hard decisions what to pack.

Fourteen degrees in Rome and cold at night.
We kid ourselves, a summer holiday,
for winter time has not yet lost its bite.

So jumpers, scarves and jackets make their way
into my case of generous proportion,
but now the sides begin to bulge and splay.

And what about my time upon the ocean
when I have to dress up posh to go to dine?
And will I need the bathers, hat and lotion,

assuming summer's made it by that time?
Choice has always been my tacit slogan
depending on this Greek and Latin clime.

Then on we'll go to Wales and up to Snowdon
to see the mountain, or maybe just the rain
or the possibility of mist unbroken,

nothing much to see, then down again.
So I must consider sleet and snow and wind.
The case's zip is showing signs of strain.

For travel broadens more than just the mind
and I still don't know just what to leave behind.

Gone to See Ships

25 February 2017

He has gone to see ships,
my man of the sea.
At Outer Harbour
P&O's *Aurora* will arrive at dawn.

He crept out quietly before first light,
camera in hand
and wanderlust in his eyes.

In my eyes there is only sleep,
and a dull ache in my head.

Next week I will see her.
Next week I will rise before dawn,
close the suitcase on all things
remembered and forgotten.

Head for the airport
and to Sydney.
From there to Circular Quay
where *Aurora* will be waiting

to take us on the second half
of the circumnavigation
of the world
half a century after the first.

She will take us east
across the Tasman to New Zealand.
North-east to the Pacific Islands
and off the edge of the map.

I am hoping and praying
that the flat-earthers
got it wrong.

Around the void to the other side,
across the warp in time
where east meets west.

Dropping into Hawaii,
down the coast of California
and Mexico
to the home of the Mayans.

Through the Panama Canal,
across the Caribbean and Atlantic
to St Lucia, Barbados and the Azores
and on to the motherland.

But that is next week's dream.
Meanwhile, I need to do
more practical things.

I need to wash and mend, pack and worry.
Make long lists and tick off tasks.
Say numerous goodbyes.

Prepare my home and garden
for others to occupy and tend.

Prepare myself
for this momentous journey:
new places, new people
and an awful lot of water.

The Hand of a Mayan Child

Panajachel Village, Guatamala, April 2017

High in the mountains of Guatemala.
I held the hand of a Mayan child,
the trusting touch of an ancient civilisation.

Held in her bloodline, is the knowledge
of ancient numbers and calendars.

Her forefathers were the
builders of ziggurats and temples,
the keepers of stories.

The women hold the knowledge of
colour and loom, heddle and dye
in brightly woven and embroidered cloths.

Rich culture, rich colours.
All will be hers, passed down,
centuries of tradition, years of practice,
hours of toil.

This land is blessed with beauty and bounty:
good rainfall, rich volcanic soils,
fields of sugar cane and coffee,
acres of bananas.

Regimented rows of grey-spined pineapples,
mangoes and papaya growing
along the village lanes.

The Mayan men labour
no longer to build their temples,
but over the harvest,
breaking their backs in the cane fields.

The women stoop over their looms
as they have for centuries,
but now they vie for the tourist dollar.

I am guilty, here in Panajachel
seeking my bargains
in beads, bags and blankets
to decorate my first world life,
forgetting the mother's hands,
the weeks of toil
that made these exquisite things.

But who gets rich?

Not the local Mayan people.
They live in grinding poverty
in tiny houses of cinder block,
peeling paint and rusty roofs,
at the sides of broken, dusty roads
littered with rubbish.

And dotted in between the villages
are grand mansions
behind high gates and armed guards.

The Spanish conquistadors are gone
but Guatemala is enslaved instead
by corrupt politicians and greedy tourists,
foreign land owners and drug cartels.

And we dare to wonder
why there is crime and civil unrest
in such a beautiful land.

I held the hand of a Mayan child.
Who will hold her future?

So Hard to Stop

Travelling the UK, July 2015

We have travelled far, from north to south,
from highland to the shore.
Been welcomed by the brogue of Scots
and climbed the mighty tors.

We have wandered Swansea's Mumbles
on a balmy summer night.
Heard Dylan's plaintive cries
against the dying of the light.

We've ferried to the Holy Isles
and frozen with the scribes.
We've walked the gorse-strewn hills,
felt blessèd and alive.

Climbed castles' spiral stairways
and sat on ancient thrones.
I've shared the seat where a poet wrote
of albatross and stone.

I've written with his quill
a tiny poem of my own
to display upon his study wall
(when I'm gone, they'll take it down).

But what I haven't told you is,
that when we've had enough,
looking for the B&B
always proves quite rough.

For Genevieve, the satnav
doesn't know the one way roads
and we do double roundabouts,
and bend the highway codes.

Then we reach our destination
in tiredness and dismay,
for the closest legal parking spot
is half a mile away.

Then cases trundled up the street
and up a flight or two.
Yes, we asked to have a room
that had a lovely view.

The hardest part is always
at the day's decline,
for Britain is the homeland
of the double yellow line.

For Love and Other Cruises

A rondeau, with apologies to Air Supply

For love and other cruises, he's my man
to take me round the world and understand
the joy of open seas and foreign shores,
together for so long and evermore,
as long as there is water, salt and sand.

I knew the day I met him, the demands
of his nomadic ways, of shifting sands,
of brine that fills his heart and every pore
for love and other cruises.

When younger he was skipper, I the hand,
but nowadays, we sail in ships more grand,
for with my silver sailor, I adore
the joys we share, the places we explore.

We throw the streamers, watch the farewell band,
set sail again, for ever distant lands
for love and other cruises.

Lindisfarne

May 2013

Lindisfarne, a windswept lowland,
a tourist destination
when the sea allows.

But once the tide comes in
the three-mile causeway
disappears.

The peninsula becomes an island,
a sanctuary.

The urgency is washed away
in gentle ocean ripples.

No impatience will change the tide.
The pace of life slows.
Waiting, contemplating,
seeing God in the stillness,

as St Aidan did,
the Apostle of Northumbria.

This is one of God's thin places,
where spheres touch
and heaven is glimpsed from earth.

Tourist or pilgrim?

Tickets, passports in my hand
I wait in queues on foreign land
and my identity is scanned
to see if I can stay.

And innocent, they let me pass
from airport guard to welcome glass
I want to know you, but alas
the truth is shut away.

I see just what they want me to
of hotel rooms and swimming pools.
The wealth and glitter I am shown.
Leave poverty and problems well alone.

Art and dance and music bright,
a dizzy spectacle at night
as other aspects of your plight
are hidden well away.

We take our air-conditioned rides
through river valleys, mountain sides
but all the beauty cannot hide
the lives in disarray.

I see just what they want me to
of hotel rooms and swimming pools.
The wealth and glitter I am shown.
Leave poverty and problems well alone.

Can I ever change your plight,
bring inequality to light,
or is the change beyond my sight
while I live my life this way?

Safe within my first world zone,
I stand apart, you fight alone.
Will I care when I am home
or will I turn away?

I see just what they want me to
of hotel rooms and swimming pools.
The wealth and glitter I am shown
Leave poverty and problems well alone.

Oxford

In the Great Hall of Christ Church College,
Professor Charles Dodgson,
instead of pondering quadratic equations
over his lunch,
watched the ever busy Dean Liddell,
dash down the staircase, near the head table
and imagined a white rabbit,
fob watch in hand, scurry down his burrow.

Across town, near Magdalen College,
Tolkien and Lewis joined the Inklings
and exchanged ideas on the climate of Narnia
and the topography of Middle Earth
over a pint or two in the Eagle and Child.

But back in the here and now,
the weather is closing in.

A professor, black gowned and umbrellaed
increases speed at the expense of dignity
and hastens to somewhere out of the rain.

Students on bicycles, burdened by bags of books,
seek shelter, take risks on slippery roads.
Short black gowns, practical but odd,
safe beyond the reach of spokes and chains,
billow out behind.

I have no real role in it,
safe from the weather atop a tourist bus,
a mere spectator in the world of learning,
yearning
to be more a part of its ivory-tower reality.

But it is not about reality.
It is about myth and imagination.

It is for me, mostly about C.S. Lewis,
his ability to articulate his faith
in fantasy and apologetics
where battles are won,
not by power, but through sacrifice.

Evensong in Christ Church Cathedral
raises my spirit to new heights
as human voices, unaccompanied,
rise in praise of God.

Oxford is the city of dreaming spires,
architecture and history,
beauty and magic.

The beauty of learning
the magic of imagination
and the immense potential
of the human mind and soul.

The Artisans

I have a soft spot for castles,
keeps, stone spiral staircases,
drawbridges and moats,
portcullises and fine slate floors.

I tend to pass by the cannons
and the brass monkeys,
the boiling oil and cannon fodder,
forget about the oubliette.

A narrow view
of history
I admit.

Move on instead to
grand banqueting halls
hung with fine tapestries,
to warm the cold stone,
impress the gentry,
and hide the rising damp.

An enormous hearth
with a side of beef
slowly turning on a spit
warming the bones and
whetting the appetite.

The bed chambers for
M'Lord and Lady,
with their four-poster beds
draped in velvet.

Shafts of dusty light,
prismed into colours
through the stained-glass
windows.

And what a privilege
to have
a Licence to Crenellate.

But none of it would exist
without the skill
of the architect and stonemason,
the labour of the serfs.

The carpenters and joiners,
the artisans of glass and plaster,
the weavers of fine tapestries.

I sense a little guilt
in my delight of castles,
a conflict with my
socialist ideals.

And there's the rub:
the very rich
underpaying the very talented,
the skilled labour,
the 'cheap' muscle,

to construct
these confectionery delights
that would not exist
in an egalitarian world.

Yet what lives on?
Not the rich lords
and ladies
but the work of the Artisans,
for the commoner to enjoy.

Questions of the Soul

This red dirt, you made me from this?
Mixed with living water
moulded and twisted to shape.
I bet you laughed
when you made the double helix.
Smiled
as you drew your image
in the twists.
Inscribed it
with messages and memories
and breathed me into life.
And here I am
just another ordinary miracle.

Tapestry

November 1998

Life, a multicoloured
silken thread, drawn out
from birth to death.

Work it alone,
tie it in knots,
weave a tangled web
or cut it short.

The differences are subtle,
the choice not easy.

From where we stand
it seems a clash of colours
and frayed edges.

Or, indentured
to the Master Craftsman,
make a work of art.

And when your silk is finished
you can join the Master
on the upper side
and see the images
you helped to weave.

This Light of Reason

Based on a Christmas sermon by John Donne and a composition by Nicholas O'Neil to commemorate the life of Jo Cox, a member of the British parliament who was killed for her compassion for refugees.

Take this light of reason
and light from it your candle.
Give thanks to God
for humble beginnings.

See in that light, your Saviour in a stable,
his mother in heavenly obedience
and earthly shame.

Understand the sacrifice of Son,
mother and earthly father.

Watch their flight to Egypt
and see in them the refugees
that travel homeless in our world.

Watch him heal and comfort
yet live his life with nowhere to rest
his weary head.

Follow him into the garden.
Stay with him a while
in prayer and grief
for a damaged world.

Do not deny him
as he is whipped
and hung upon a tree.

Stand by and share
his mother's tears.

Turn that faint light inward.
See your own soul
and let the light
cast out the darkness.

For when the bright fire
of worldly man
has burnt itself
to ash,

that tiny flame,
lit from the light of Christ,
the light of reason and compassion,

will show you pearls of great wisdom
and warm and guide you
to eternal life.

The Depth of Unknowing

You are to me, Lord,
like the mighty ocean,
in width and depth
and magnitude.

Beyond my understanding.
Awesome in your beauty
and your power.

Never tamed.

A source of life,
but death
is never far away.

We underestimate you
at our peril.

I am held in thrall
and I can know you not.

But do you know me
any better, Lord,
than the ocean knows
a grain of sand?

To Grasp the Infinite

I call him Father
and stand accused
of personifying
God.

I admit the deed,
but claim
my innocence.

For God, himself,
saw fit
to do the same.

Humanity
is far too small
to grasp the infinite.

And knowing
that the written Word
had left us wanting

He clothed the Word
in flesh, and sent
the Son of Man.

The Passion of the Trinity

Easter 1995

All three walked the road to Golgotha

All three felt the rough wood
against his ravaged back.

All three lay down together
as the nails were hammered in
and felt the sinews and the bone tear
as he was lifted up.

Blood and sweat mingled
and stung his eyes,
closing their window on the world.

Each breath was an effort,
ribs stretched and lungs unable to fill.

They shared the pain
and comforted one another.

'It is time,' said the Spirit.
The Father broke the bonds.
The Son cried out in anguish
for he was now alone.

He whispered, 'It is finished,'
and he breathed his last.

The Spirit wept, her tears rolling
like great storm clouds over the earth,
blotting out the sun.

The Father roared in grief
and the earth trembled.
He rent his garment
and the curtain of the temple tore in two.

Each now in their isolation,
weighing the sorrow of the world.

The soul fell out of reach.
So it would stay until the third day…
and each day was like a thousand years.

The Precious Gem

It is sought
in Swiss bank vaults,
on streamlined yachts
or windswept shores.

Others search
in famous restaurants,
exclusive hotels,
in fashion, food or fame,

within the arts,
the accolades of others.

It is sought in bottles,
pills and needles.
It is not there.

It grew over years
in a tiny prison cell
on Robben Island.

It was sought in the garden
of Gethsemane,
found in the slums of Calcutta,
the quiet highlands of Nepal.

Serenity
resides within;
rests not in position or possession,
but in the mind and heart.

Apples and Snakes

With thanks to Bishop Arthur Malcolm

He smiled, my friend Arthur,
the first Aboriginal bishop,
as he shared this little
piece of wisdom, over dinner.

'If Adam and Eve had been
Aboriginal,' he said,
'the world would be a better place,

for they would not
have been tempted by the apple.
They would have eaten the snake.'

And maybe that did happen
some forty thousand years ago.

Perhaps there was an Eve Nabaljarri
and an Adam Jagamarra
who salivated at the smell
of snake meat cooking
over an open fire,

while the fruit of knowledge
hung, ignored, uneaten,
upon the tree.
Knowledge lost,
but innocence retained.

Insecurities and Doubts

Anxieties surface, beads of sweat
crazing the surface as they crystallise.
Salt on base metal,
corroding, not preserving,
the very thing I cherish.

Blemishes

Sure, there is beauty in the smooth bark,
but lumps and bumps grow new branches.
The stretched round belly bears the child.

Old skin holds the wisdom and the wine.
Scars may tell of courage and of passion
or maybe just of misadventure.

Forget perfection;
it is not the stuff of life.

No Pictures Please

For Martin, who always seems to be there with his camera

No pictures please.
They cause such consternation.
So much crueller than the bathroom mirror.
So much harsher with flash and shadow
to emphasise the imperfections,
widening the chasm
between fact and delusion.

Hide those images away.
They are too raw.
A decade at least,
in a cool dark place
to mature like good wine,
grow the patina of nostalgia,
the kudos of antiquity.

With the detachment of time
we'll be able to say,
'Remember those days?
What a blast we had,
and we didn't look half bad
for fifty-something.'

Always the Bridesmaid

For John Pfitzner and his Auslan poem, 2012 (John died soon after in January 2013, so I never had the chance to share this with him)

As a kid in school
I was really good at coming second.

I missed out on the main role
in the school play.
'Excellent reading,' they said,
'but perhaps the wrong stature.'
Why didn't they just say,
'You're too short.'

No second prizes
in the debating team either.

Then there was the coming second
at job interviews,
which is exactly the same
as coming last.

And now they tell me
I almost won
'Poet of the Month'.

Dragging up
the same old feelings
of not quite good enough.

But I had to admit
your winning entry was a gem.

So John,
just throw me the bouquet!

Self e-steam

What a luxury
is the morning shower,
washing away bad dreams
and gastronomic indiscretions.

Softening skin,
hardening resolve,
smoothing wrinkles,
fading age spots.

Scars, years and kilos
sloughed off
like snakeskin
down the drain.

Then swathed in towel,
smile
at the soft-focus me
in the misty mirror.

And, as long as I avoid
reflection,
I can bask in illusion
all the day.

Hollow

I am all on the outside.
Hung up on appearances,
approval.

Thin skin, brittle shell.
All the promise
of an Easter egg.

Sweet, inviting.
Inside, nothing.

Do I exist at all
when I'm alone?

Islands of Humanity

Islands
in a sea of insecurities.
Not knowing
the thoughts of others.

Wanting to belong,
but always staying
just apart from the melee,
watching, judging,
alone in the crowd.

Smile fixed.
Hands safe around a glass.

The relief of recognition
of a familiar face.
A brief respite.

Readjust the smile.
Air kiss with the host.
'What a lovely party!'

Insecurities

I trust you implicitly
I think…

What I don't trust is my own ability
to attract you, to delight you and to hold.
Anxieties surface, beads of sweat
crazing the surface as they crystallise.

Salt on base metal,
corroding, not preserving,
the very thing I cherish.

You say you love me
and I love you with a passion.

Why can't I just accept that
and enjoy?

Resignation

1 July 1998 to the worst boss ever

You abuse your power
and ranking, at my cost
and tempt me by example
to free my darker side.

I have become too well acquainted
with my anger, never vented,
and find I understand
the cause of violence in our world.

You buy my skill too cheaply
and sell it off too high
with never thanks or credit
where it's due.

You have stolen time and talent,
bruised my confidence and pride.
So I am leaving.

I'll go hungry
before I let you further
wound my soul.

When you are away

When you are away
my head is heavy
in a cloud of apathy.

Weighted, waiting,
hours and days, wasting.

There seems no purpose
when you are away.

Routines carry on.
I go to work, I answer phones.
I laugh in company, go home alone.

And no one else need know
or shall be told
that inside, inside, I am on hold…

When you are away.

Each day is a gift

A cliché I know,
but only so, because it's true.

How many of them have I wasted?
Left unwrapped,
hidden under the blankets
or buried in busyness.

How many forgotten?
No thank you or gratitude
to the giver.

They were taken for granted
when they were aplenty,
but now there is
a limited supply.

Knowing them rare and irreplaceable
what has changed?
I still don't know how
to use them well.

Living in the Shade

February 2017

I am living in the shade
of the tall poppies,
too far down
for the accolades
to filter through.

But also protected
from the bright lights,
the glare of criticism,
the savage bite
of the voracious hounds.

I live in sympathy
for the tall poppies.
The air is too thin up there
for them to catch their breath.

Every word they utter is at risk
of being twisted, sharpened
and turned against them.

When the hounds come
to cut them down,
when the shade is gone
and the glare is on us,
will we all shrivel
in the heat
of one another's jealousy?

I am grateful to the tall poppies.
Let us prune carefully,
for it is safer in their shade.

On the Lighter Side

In humour we try to hide
and in so doing reveal ourselves.

Buying Local

I've been down to the market
and bought myself a treat.
It is a pretty dainty thing
and the price was really neat.

So I thought I'd buy another one
and help the local trade.
They come in many sizes
and many different shades.

I wore one to a party
and I thought I looked a dream,
but when I took it off that night
my skin had turned to green.

I scrubbed and scrubbed myself
with soap and suds galore.
Now my skin is sore and tingly,
but at least it's green no more.

So back next week to market
to get my money back
and whinge about the quality
or its total lack.

But no one'd even heard of her.
The owner had shot through.
And I'll never wear the other one
in case it turns me blue.

The Modem and I

I arrived at work this morning, and dismay.
Not a single email has arrived since some time yesterday.

It could be no one's talking or wants our sound advice.
Far more likely though, there's a fault with some device.

I check the files to see who sold us our access,
then phone the friendly Optus man to help me with this mess.

I wait awhile and listen while they tell me several times
'You're such a valued customer, so please just hold the line.'

Eventually I hear a voice and I can tell that he
is underneath a whirring fan in Mumbai or New Delhi.

'Is it you or me?' I ask. I haven't got a clue.
'Your modem's probably in a twist, so I think it might be you.'

'Turn the modem off and on,' the standard IT line,
'give it twenty seconds rest and then it should be fine.'

All very well for him, I moan, this won't be picturesque,
as the power point for the modem is underneath my desk.

So while I'm crawling underneath with my bum stuck in the air,
the boss walks in and all he sees is an ample derrière.

I rise too suddenly and hit my head along the way.
'Hide and seek?' he laughs. 'Can anybody play?'

Rubbing my head, I find the phone and the patient IT man.
'What now?' I ask 'Well, now.' he says, 'the lights should all be on.'

'Well, no,' I say, 'no red, no orange, no green,
not a light of any colour, so what does all this mean?'

'Don't panic,' he replies in a condescending tone,
'I think you may have forgotten to turn the modem on.'

And so I did… and it's all the boss's fault,
and my dignity takes another hit as I reach the power point.

This time I am rewarded with the friendly blinking lights
and thirty-something emails come dashing from the night.

The boss looks on, and things don't seem so funny
'I'll put the kettle on,' he says. 'I think I owe you coffee.'

'And that's not all,' I say, landing on my sword.
'How about some petty cash for a nice new power board?'

Oh, I Wish I Hadn't Eaten That

Oh, I wish I hadn't eaten that,
all those calories and all that fat.

For years, those meats and cheeses
in thee I put my trust!
Now the measurement around my waist,
that used to be my bust.

And as for thighs, I don't remember
eating all that orange peel.
no more bathing suits for me
or skimpy shorts that might reveal.

So I'm trying to go all vegan;
save the chickens, cows and lambs,
eating seaweed and buck wheat
and umeboshi plums.

Why am I not endeared
to broccoli and peas,
spinach and bok choy
and gritty soy cheese?

Well, the damage wasn't overnight,
so can't fix it in a day.
Perhaps a tiny slice of cake
to see me on my way.

Exotics

Early Saturday morning, the gardening guru on the radio keeps referring to introduced plants as 'exotics'. His tone is most disparaging. All I can visualise is a group of young girls, scantily dressed, with their long legs seductively wrapped around poles.

They seem well behaved in summer,
hanging around in parks, offering shade
over other people's picnics,
dropping sticks for dogs to chase.

In autumn when the barbecues are over,
they change their attire,
strut their stuff in reds, oranges and yellows,
a little showy but nothing too offensive.

Then the change of character comes,
slowly, teasingly, shedding their clothes,
strains of 'Big Spender' heard faintly
in the winter air.

Then they hang around street corners,
waving their bony fingers at kerb crawlers,
an affront to decent law-abiding citizens.

Spring comes and they dress in little-girl pink,
soft greens and shades of copper,
assuming a degree of coy modesty, and hoping we'll
forgive their winter indiscretions.

On the Soapbox

I want another podium
and I want it now!
(with apologies to Roald Dahl)

The Den

Inspired by a series of paintings and sketches of foxes
by Ross Morgan (SALA, Adelaide Arcade, August 2015)

Huddled together in the den
you stare at us, the intruders.
Both fear and challenge flare
in those vulpine eyes.

We malign you when you hunt,
you killers of quolls and lambs.

But we brought you here,
stole you from your home
on the other side of the world,
for our own sport, the sport of kings.

You are both beautiful and dangerous,
rank yet glorious, with your russet fur
and trophy tails.

I wish for you a simpler,
safer life than this,
condemned to be
both hunter and hunted.

Carbon Footprint

Over Heathrow,
blue skies,
where planes
score the air
with condensation trails.

A criss-cross tapestry of scars,
some soft and faded
by time and wind.
Others fresh, thin, sharp.

The restlessness
of a thousand travellers like me
stamping our carbon footprints
on the planet we claim to love
and self-harming the sky.

Best We Forget

11 November 2015

He is home now
safe from IEDs and guns,
the grit of sand, the smell of blood.
Enemies who wear no uniform.

There are no scars
or bruises on his skin.
He lived his war unscathed,
or so he thought.

But the windows of his soul
are clouded over
from all the things
they've seen.

The gates and bars
all tightly locked,
the guilt and horror
of surviving, caged inside.

A wild, frightened animal
that lashes out
at those who get too close.
The wounds are there,
unseen, unhealed
and spreading like contagion
to everything and everyone
he loves.

You Are Homeless

You are homeless.
And whose fault is that?

You say your father
came home on pay day
with beer in his belly
and anger in his fists.

Until he didn't come at all.

And your mother worked all hours
so you never bothered to ask her
to help you with your homework.

Do you remember
not concentrating in school
just because you had
no breakfast in your belly?

And the teachers who
didn't notice or didn't care
that you never really
learnt to read.

You say the system
is too hard to follow,
the forms too hard
to understand.

Whose fault is that?

Perhaps next time
you could pick your parents
and your neighbourhood
more carefully.

Questions of the Night

Hyde Park, Sydney, 2002

'Go home now,' say the wise,
'and hide,
for Hyde Park
is no place for a lady
after dark.'

But why?

Is the dark
more evil than the day
when bats are aloft
and pigeons have gone away?

But where?

On the bench sits a man
with a bushy beard.
I'm sure he didn't have it
when the sun was here.

He grew it just now
to frighten me.

But how?

Well, it hasn't worked
and I still want the right
to enjoy the park
past the evening light.

But I won't remain.
I'll go and hide
in my safe little room
on the seventh floor.

Go out no more.

For if something happens
the wise will exclaim,
'Well, she asked for it!'

But I don't remember when.

Upon the Merest Hint

A rondeau

They listen for a hint upon the air
of indiscretions, signs of an affair,
invading others' lives and privacy
to titillate the likes of you and me
in media where honesty is rare.

Like Chinese whispers, floating on the air,
destroying truth and building on despair,
the paparazzi weave their fantasies
upon the merest hint.

Relationships are torn beyond repair.
Suspicion borne from words that hardly bear
an element of true reality.
Chinese whispers spread by you and me,
half-truths passed on without a thought or care
upon the merest hint.

Semaphore, the End of the Line

6 July 2015

A glorious winter's day
with blue sky, warm sun
and a gentle ocean breeze.
The train is running,
and here at the end of the line
the kiosk is doing a brisk trade
in ice cream and chips.

The children's park is abuzz.
School holidays and sunshine
have filled the place.
All the young ones play together,
squealing, laughing, climbing,
running, swinging, sliding.

May this not be the end of the line
for children of a certain age,
when some sage feels obliged
to let them know
who is alright to play with,
and who is not.

Parents watch, clad in everything from
board shorts to burkas,
track pants to turbans.

God smiles. It warms any parent's heart
to see the children play together well.

Margaret Clark spent a nomadic childhood in England, Scotland and Ireland before emigrating at age ten to South Australia. After school and college in SA, she married and moved to the Northern Territory supposedly for three years, but staying for thirty. She worked as a teacher in remote Aboriginal communities, raised two children and later retrained in the field of architectural drafting and design.

A move to Brisbane prompted another life change, working for the Anglican Church and doing part-time theology studies.

Retirement brought her and husband Nigel back to South Australia and proximity to their growing family.

The nomadic nature of childhood has not left her and retirement has brought opportunities for travel which has been the inspiration for many of the poems in this collection and also brought reflection on the joys of home.

Her poetry has been published in several anthologies by Friendly Street Poets, The Eremos Institute and the *Guardian Magazine* of the Anglican Diocese of Adelaide. Some of her work has also been set to music and performed at the Toowoomba Christian Music Symposium and in churches in Queensland and South Australia.

She is a committee member of Friendly Street Poets, a poets' collective for the writing, reading and publishing of poetry in South Australia, and was co-editor for their 2016 anthology *Many Eyes, Many Voices*.

Tourist or Pilgrim? is her second book. Her first poetry collection, *Frayed Edges*, was published by Ginninderra Press in 2016.

www.ingramcontent.com/pod-product-compliance
Lightning Source LLC
Chambersburg PA
CBHW070918080526
44589CB00013B/1343